EAT GREEN

Anita Yasuda

www.av2books.com

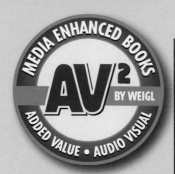

AV² by Weigl brings you media enhanced books that support active learning.

AV² provides enriched content that supplements and complements this book. Weigl's AV² books strive to create inspired learning and engage young minds for a total learning experience.

Go to **www.av2books.com**, and enter this book's unique code. You will have access to video, audio, web links, quizzes, a slide show, and activities.

BOOK CODE

R116836

Audio
Listen to sections of the book read aloud.

Video

Web Link
Find research sites and play interactive games.

Try This!
Complete activities and hands-on experiments.

Due to the dynamic nature of the Internet, some of the URLs and activities provided as part of AV² by Weigl may have changed or ceased to exist. AV² by Weigl accepts no responsibility for any such changes. All media enhanced books are regularly monitored to update addresses and sites in a timely manner. Contact AV² by Weigl at 1-866-649-3445 or av2books@weigl.com with any questions, comments, or feedback.

Published by AV² by Weigl
350 5ᵗʰ Avenue, 59ᵗʰ Floor
New York, NY 10118
Web site: www.av2books.com   www.weigl.com

Library of Congress Cataloging-in-Publication Data available upon request.
Fax 1-866-44-WEIGL for the attention of the Publishing Records department.

ISBN 978-1-61690-091-5 (hard cover)
ISBN 978-1-61690-092-2 (soft cover)

Printed in the United States of America in North Mankato, Minnesota
2 3 4 5 6 7 8 9 0 15 14 13 12 11

122011
WEP081211

Project Coordinators: Heather C. Hudak, Robert Famighetti
Design: Terry Paulhus
Project Editor: Emily Dolbear
Photo Research: Edward A. Thomas
Layout and Production: Tammy West

Every reasonable effort has been made to trace ownership and to obtain permission to reprint copyright material. The publishers would be pleased to have any errors or omissions brought to their attention so that they may be corrected in subsequent printings.

Weigl acknowledges Getty Images as its primary image supplier for this title.

CONTENTS

MAKING THE WORLD A GREENER PLACE

How can you make the world a greener place? You can help the planet by reducing your **carbon footprint**. A carbon footprint is the measure of **greenhouse gases** produced by human activities.

Greenhouse gases are created by burning **fossil fuels**. People burn fossil fuels for electricity, heating, and powering vehicles. One of the biggest causes of climate change is the greenhouse gas known as **carbon dioxide**. Many scientists believe that carbon **emissions** are more damaging to Earth than any other kind of pollution.

There are many ways you can reduce your carbon footprint. One way is to walk or ride your bike instead of riding in a car. You can turn off lights when you leave a room to reduce energy waste. Reusing plastic shopping bags to carry other items is another way to help the environment. You can **recycle** newspaper so that fewer trees are chopped down to make new paper.

WHAT IS EATING GREEN?

Eating green is one of the ways you can help make the world a greener place. Making a decision to eat green food at home can lower your carbon footprint. Eating green is about what you buy to eat and drink, when you buy foods, how you cook them, and even how you dispose of food waste. From reusable shopping bags to planting your own edible garden, eating green means buying local produce and making wise choices.

Think about what you ate for lunch. Do you know where the ingredients came from? How far did the ingredients travel before you ate them? Was the food in reusable, recyclable containers? What did you do with the waste? These are just a few factors to consider when eating green.

1 LOOKING TO THE FUTURE

W hen people produce, process, buy, sell, and prepare food, they must do it in a way that least affects the environment. By understanding their role in the food chain, people can make better choices. They can encourage producers and manufacturers to use resources wisely and less wastefully.

WAYS TO CHOOSE
ECO-FRIENDLY FOOD

Rotate Crops

Farmers who **rotate** crops are practicing **sustainability**. Since Roman times, farmers have grown a series of different crops on the same land to help keep the soil productive. Rotating crops allows the land to recover nutrients, prevents soil erosion, and reduces the need for **fertilizer**. A 2006 study found that crop rotation helps increase yields by almost 80 percent.

Preserve a Diversity of Seeds

In the United States, the National Plant Germplasm System (NPGS) has one of the world's largest **gene** banks. Preserving genetic material, such as seeds or plant cuttings, from different crops is important. Crop variety helps researchers improve plant traits, such as the ability to survive pests, diseases, and environmental stresses. The result can be improved crop quality and productivity.

Buy Fair Trade

Buying **fair trade** products is one way to support a sustainable food system. The goal of this market-based program is to pay producers in developing countries fair prices and to promote sustainable farming practices. A food that has the fair trade label means that it has met certain economic, social, and green rules. Fair trade food is grown without harmful chemicals. In the United States, coffee, tea, and chocolate may be fair trade products. Of the foods you eat, what could you replace with fair trade products?

"People power can help bring about a revolution in the way food is produced and sold."

–Hilary Benn, British cabinet member

2 EATING LOCAL

Most meals in the United States have ingredients from at least five other countries. People are shipping food farther than ever. For every mile (kilometer) that food travels, energy is used to make, transport, and store it. This traveling, called **food miles**, produces pollution. Sustainable agriculture works best when people eat food grown near their communities.

WAYS TO SUPPORT LOCALLY GROWN FOOD

Buy from Farmers' Markets

An Iowa State University study showed that food typically travels between 1,500 and 3,000 miles (2,414 and 3,219 kilometers) from farm to plate. Buying local is the best way to lower the greenhouse gas emissions produced when food is shipped. Almost 5,000 farmers' markets operate in the United States. What could you buy from a local farmer?

> "Eating locally isn't just a fad—it may be one of the most important ways we save ourselves and the planet."
>
> –*David Suzuki, environmental scientist*

Take Part in Community Supported Agriculture or a Food Cooperative

Community supported agriculture (CSA) is a partnership between a community and a farmer. Individuals buy shares in the crop a farm produces. They receive a box of fruits and vegetables each week during the farming season. In this way, growers and consumers share the risks and benefits of growing

and harvesting food. Today, thousands of CSA farms produce vegetables, fruit, eggs, milk, and poultry in the United States. A **food cooperative (co-op)** is a grocery store run by its members. What are the benefits of being in a co-op or a CSA?

Walk This Way

Walking, riding a bike, and even carpooling to the grocery store cuts down on pollution. What farms and markets could you reach by foot or on a bike to help lower your carbon footprint?

EATING IN
SEASON

Eating green means paying attention to the seasons. For years, the demand for out-of-season produce in the United States has been growing. Shipping out-of-season produce creates pollutants that add to **global warming**. By eating seasonal foods, people reduce the energy needed to ship the foods people eat.

WAYS TO REDUCE THE NEED FOR TRANSPORTING FOOD

Find Out What Is Fresh Near You

Fruits and vegetables that travel long distances are harvested before they are ripe. Sometimes, farm operations use chemical treatments to make the produce last longer. All over the United States, u-pick farms give people the chance to pick their own fruits and vegetables. The Natural Resources Defense Council has a search engine that lists local produce available each season. Oranges, apples, and avocadoes are examples of food grown in the United States. What kind of produce grows near you?

> "To restore balance to our planet, reduce our carbon footprint, and to maintain optimum health, we must eat locally sourced food—and that means, Eating in Season!"
>
> –Kerry Dunnington, caterer and author

Look for Carbon Labeling

Some companies measure the amount of carbon dioxide given off at each stage of production. The challenge is to lower the effect food production has on climate change. In the United States, major companies are studying how to reduce carbon emissions during the creation of their products. No countrywide standard exists yet.

Cut Down on Shipped Food

According to a U.S. organization called the National Sustainable Agriculture Information Service (ATTRA), 80 percent of all energy used by the food system is from shipping, processing, home refrigeration, and preparation. Only 20 percent of energy is used in production. Shipping food by plane, ship, truck, or train increases global warming. Air shipping creates the most carbon dioxide. Foods such as pineapples, cheese, and papayas are often shipped by air. What foods could you avoid eating to lower your carbon footprint?

4 GROWING YOUR OWN
FOOD

Eating green encourages people to make wise decisions. Planting an edible garden is one way to lower a person's carbon footprint. A garden reduces the need for packaging and transportation. It also provides fresh seasonal produce. Even the White House has a garden. It grows 60 kinds of fruits and vegetables.

WAYS TO GROW YOUR OWN FOOD

Check out the WhoFarm Due to the efforts of the nonprofit White House **Organic** Farm Project (WhoFarm), an edible garden grows on the White House lawn. The garden uses **compost** collected from the White House, the Capitol, and the Supreme Court as fertilizer. Some of the food is delivered by bicycle to schools and to homeless people in Washington, D.C. The farm has its own school bus called the WhoFarmMobile, which has visited schools across the country.

Try Organic Pest Control Green gardens promote healthy soil and plant life. They do not use **pesticides** or other chemicals. They use natural methods, such as fertilizing, hand weeding, and insect predators, such as ladybugs. Honeybees and butterflies are helpful, too. They pollinate many crop plants.

"[E]mpowering people to secure food for themselves and for their family in a sustainable way is central to a human rights approach to the food crisis."

–Louise Arbour, former UN High Commissioner for Human Rights

Help at a Community Garden

A **community garden** allows families to grow their own fruits and vegetables on common land. Gardens improve air quality. They lower family food costs and encourage community activity. GreenThumb, the largest U.S. community gardening program, supports more than 600 gardens in New York City. How can you begin a community garden in your area? What would you grow? How would you divide the food?

5 ORGANIC STANDARDS

The number of consumers of green goods in the United States has grown. The United States Department of Agriculture (USDA) develops and administers the national standards for organic manufacturers and producers. The USDA determines which foods can be labeled organic.

WAYS TO MONITOR GREEN FARMING PRACTICES

Create Uniform Standards

The USDA's National Organic Program (NOP) regulates the standards for any farm, wild crop harvesting, or handling operation that wants to sell agricultural products labeled as organic. The standards encourage growers to

conserve soil and water. Since the 1990s, federal and state support has increased. Organic crop insurance, research, education, and marketing are improving. How many fresh foods in your grocery store are labeled organic?

Look for USDA Organic Seals

After passage of the Organic Foods Production Act (OFPA) in 1990, the U.S. Congress asked the USDA to develop national standards for organic agricultural products. Now, goods labeled organic must come from certified farms or companies. Consumers who want to buy organic foods can look for the seal. Labels are based on the percentage of organic ingredients in a product. In the United States, organic goods account for more than three percent of total food sales.

> "My wish is for you to have a strong, sustainable movement to educate every child about food, to inspire families to cook again, and to empower people everywhere to fight obesity."
>
> –*Jamie Oliver, chef and author*

Farm Green

Conserving fossil fuels and making food without using chemicals is called farming green. Green farms do not give **antibiotics** or growth **hormones** to their livestock. Their meat, poultry, eggs, and dairy products are free of these chemicals. Green farming is one of the fastest-growing areas of U.S. agriculture. By 2005, all 50 states had certified organic farmland. California has the most licensed operations. Where is your closest organic farm?

6 REDUCING KITCHEN WASTE

Throwing away food wastes the energy used to produce, package, and ship it. The average U.S. family spends almost $600 each year on food that is thrown in the garbage. Some researchers believe that cutting back on food waste could lessen the impact on the environment by as much as 25 percent.

WAYS TO CUT DOWN ON FOOD WASTE

Make a Plan Buy only what you need. Planning meals with a shopping list is a sensible way to help reduce waste. Checking use-by dates in the store on perishable items, such as meat, eggs, and dairy products, helps reduce waste later. According to the USDA, Americans discard about 96 billion pounds (44 billion kilograms) of food each year. How much food do you throw away in a week? How could you reduce this waste? Does having a list affect your choices? How could you use lists in other areas of your life to reduce waste?

Store Food Properly Learning how to store food properly cuts down on waste. Green kitchens use eco-friendly stainless steel, glass, and even wood containers instead of plastic, which some scientists say takes 1,000 years to break down. How could you store plastic-wrapped items in your refrigerator in a more eco-friendly way?

Compost Your Waste
Partially decomposed plant material used to enrich the soil is called compost. People use compost to prevent soil erosion and provide plants with nutrients. Seattle was the first U.S. city that required residents to compost food waste. How can you collect compost at home?

"Composting your food scraps is probably the single most effective thing you can do as a citizen in the United States today."
–*Jared Blumenfeld, San Francisco city environmental officer*

7 GREENER PACKAGING

The less packaging a product uses, the more green it is. Packaging with recycled and **biodegradable** materials creates less waste. Less energy is used to make these types of packaging.

WAYS TO REDUCE PACKAGING WASTE

Limit Packaging
A product's primary packaging is what the consumer handles. About 70 percent of all primary packaging is used for food and drink. In a 2009 Ipsos Marketing study, consumers said they would give up convenient packaging for greener choices. Fruits and vegetables bought loose and buying in bulk cut down on waste. What products in your home have too much packaging? What has minimal packaging?

Recycle and Reuse
Being green means avoiding goods that cannot be composted or recycled. In a green kitchen, bottles, tubs, and containers are reused or recycled. Recycling lowers the need for **landfills**, saves energy, and lowers greenhouse gas emissions, which add to global warming. What can you recycle?

Bring Your Own Bag
Americans use more than 380 billion plastic bags, sacks, and wraps each year. Only about two percent of plastic bags in the United States are recycled. Some litter roads. Others are found in water and kill marine life. The rest are sent to landfills. How could you encourage people to bring their own bags when they go food shopping?

Improve Designs
Every year, the chemical giant DuPont awards companies for their innovative green packaging. Recent winners include bakeware and gift cartons made from completely **renewable**, compostable, or biodegradable material. Corn, switch grass, and grain are renewable resources used to make biodegradable goods, such as eco-friendly utensils.

"Waste is a tax on the whole people."
–Albert W. Atwood, financial author

8 WATER CONSCIOUS

Green consumers make choices every day about what they eat and drink. This means choosing drinks that have the least effect on the environment. Compared to soda cans, juice boxes, and water bottles, which require packaging and shipping, tap water has the smallest carbon footprint. Did you know that about 40 percent of bottled water started out as tap water?

WAYS TO CONSERVE
FOR THE FUTURE

Drink Tap Water Instead of Bottled Water

The United States is the world's largest bottled water market. Americans recycle less than 15 percent of their water bottles. The country also has some of the world's safest tap water. The Environmental Protection Agency (EPA) sets water standards and requires water suppliers to provide annual quality reports. The U.S. Conference of Mayors in 2008 passed a motion to phase out bottled water in city buildings. Some leaders have urged restaurants to serve only tap water. How can you encourage people to drink more tap water?

"Drinking tap water instead of bottled water is not just easier on your wallet: it's also easier on the environment."

–Michael Bloomberg, mayor of New York City

Eliminate Dining Hall Trays

Dining halls can save water by not using food trays. The University of Illinois eliminated trays in one of its dining halls. This meant trays no longer needed to be washed, saving 516 gallons (1,953 liters) of water each day, a total of 110,940 gallons (419,954 L) per year. Students wasted 40 percent less food because they could not carry as much.

Conserve Water

The average American family of four uses 400 gallons (1,514 L) of water each day. Water is not an unlimited resource. Small changes to the amount of water a family uses can save a large amount of water. People can turn off the tap while brushing their teeth, scrape dishes instead of rinsing them, and limit their showers. What are other ways people can use less water?

9 HEALTHY KIDS PROGRAM

Healthful and nutritious food is an important part of eating green. First Lady Michelle Obama brought attention to eating well with her "Let's Move program." The program's key goals are to give families nutritional information, to offer healthful food at schools, to ask children to exercise, and to make healthful food available to everyone.

WAYS TO HELP SCHOOLS
EAT GREEN

Take on the Healthier School Challenge

Food quality and exercise are two parts of the HealthierUS School Challenge (HUSSC). The USDA established the program in 2004 to promote nutrition and physical activity across the country. Schools enrolled in the challenge serve meals that have more fruits, vegetables, and whole grains and less sugar, saturated fats, and sodium. Schools are encouraged to buy from co-ops. How many servings of fruits and vegetables do you eat each week at school?

Plant a School Garden

School gardens bring students together. Students can learn about how food is grown. USDA funding is available to schools that increase student and staff access to fresh fruits and vegetables. In California, $15 million dollars of funding is available to schools interested in starting or maintaining a garden program. Does your school have a garden? Who tends it when school is not in session?

"We want our children to eat right, not just because it's the right thing to do but because quite frankly healthy good food tastes good and we want them to experience that."
–Michelle Obama, First Lady of the United States

Think Farm to School

The National Farm to School Network brings food from local farms to schoolchildren nationwide. Students learn more about growing food on a farm and healthful eating habits. The network also minimizes the environmental impact of transporting the food. Where does the food at your school come from?

10 ENERGY EFFICIENT

Producing, packaging, transporting, and disposing food requires energy. Energy is also used when food is stored. Much of this energy comes from fossil fuels. Choosing food that requires less energy is part of eating green.

WAYS TO IMPROVE ENERGY EFFICIENCY

Use Climate Friendly Systems

Green growers are investing in renewable energy sources, such as solar and wind power, to reduce greenhouse gases. In 2009, the U.S. National Arboretum, with help from Alfred State College students, installed a solar-powered irrigation system that lowered energy costs, conserved resources, and reduced its carbon footprint. An arboretum is a living museum where plants grow for scientific and educational purposes.

> "I have always admired and respected plants. They are the ultimate solar collectors."
>
> –John Anderson, *president of Alfred State College*

Choose to Eat Less Meat

The United Nations Food and Agriculture Organization estimates that the livestock industry produces more greenhouse gas emissions than the transportation industry. The **methane** that livestock and their manure produce is part of global warming. Solutions may include improved animal nutrition to reduce methane production and special equipment to treat manure. Eating fewer meat and dairy products can help lessen the negative effects of livestock on the environment.

Make Your Kitchen Greener

The U.S. government runs the Energy Star program, which encourages consumers to replace inefficient appliances. With the help of Energy Star, Americans in 2009 saved $17 billion

on their utility bills and reduced greenhouse gas emissions equal to those of 30 million cars. Think of ways you could lower energy use in your home, school, or community.

10 Countries with the Most Organic Agricultural Land

Australia
about 29.7 million acres
(12 million hectares)

Argentina
about 10 million acres (4 million ha)

China
more than 2.4 million acres
(1 million ha)

United States
more than 2.4 million acres (1 million ha)

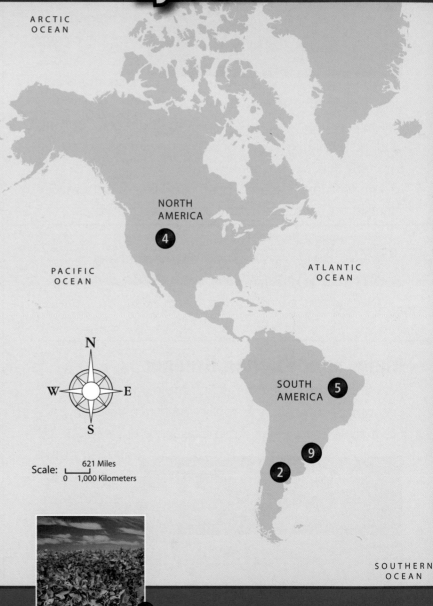

ARCTIC
OCEAN

NORTH
AMERICA
4

PACIFIC
OCEAN

ATLANTIC
OCEAN

SOUTH
AMERICA 5

9

2

N
W E
S

Scale: 621 Miles
0   1,000 Kilometers

SOUTHERN
OCEAN

Brazil
more than 2.4 million acres
(1 million ha)
5

Countries are trying to lower the environmental impact of food production. Organic agricultural land is an important part of this effort. It encourages people to look for green ways to care for the land so that there is a future in agriculture.

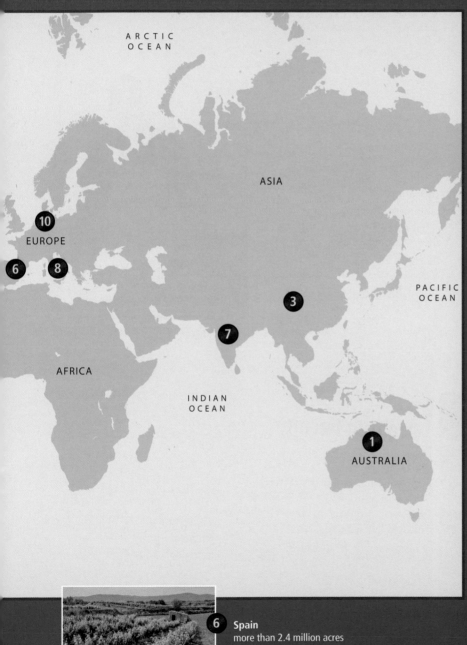

ARCTIC
OCEAN

ASIA

10 EUROPE

6   8

PACIFIC
OCEAN

7

3

AFRICA

INDIAN
OCEAN

1 AUSTRALIA

India
more than 2.4 million acres
(1 million ha)

Italy
more than 2.4 million acres
(1 million ha)

9

Uruguay
more than 2.2 million acres
(900,000 ha)

Germany
more than 2.2 million acres
(900,000 ha)

6 **Spain**
more than 2.4 million acres
(1 million ha)

Source: FiBL/IFOAM Survey 2010

Green Careers

Here are just a few green careers in the food sector.

Green Chef

Career

A green chef is responsible for a restaurant's menu, including organic ingredients and fair trade products. A green chef often buys from local farms and markets and may make special requests from them. Green chefs also help operate a green restaurant, which recycles whenever possible, composts, and uses energy efficient appliances. To-go containers are often recyclable or biodegradable. Becoming a green chef requires hard work and a commitment to buying and serving local, eco-friendly food.

Education

Chefs attend culinary school. A green chef may seek out additional organic training.

Organic Farmer

Career

Organic farmers plant, harvest, and distribute food. Conservation is of great importance to organic farmers. They plant and harvest crops without using chemical fertilizers or pesticides. Hormone-free livestock eat an organic diet. Organic agricultural standards vary from state to state. Organic farmers must work long hours, be physically strong, and enjoy learning new farming techniques.

Education

Organic farmers study agriculture at community colleges or universities. They belong to national and local organizations to develop their knowledge and skills.

What have you learned about Eating Green?

Are you a green eating expert?
Take this quiz to test your knowledge.

1 Where can you buy green food?

2 What is organic food?

3 What does it mean if a product is biodegradable?

4 What are some of the benefits of a community garden?

5 What are some green ways to go shopping?

6 What are some ways that communities can help support local farmers?

7 Why is it important to buy in season?

8 Why is drinking tap water important?

ANSWERS: 1. At a local market or farm **2.** Food produced without the use of chemicals, such as antibiotics or pesticides **3.** The item is capable of safely breaking down through the natural action for the environment or living things. **4.** A variety of fresh produce, community green space, and an improvement in the quality of life **5.** Walk, ride your bike, or carpool **6.** Buy produce directly from the farmer or support a CSA or food cooperative **7.** Food bought in season creates fewer food miles (kilometers). **8.** It is healthy and cheap, and creates no waste, unlike bottled water.

Time to Debate

ISSUE

Should school lunchrooms be required to be green?

Nearly one-third of American children are overweight or excessively overweight, also called obese. With childhood obesity on the rise in the United States, more schools are adopting healthier eating plans. In an effort to fight this problem, the U.S. government formed a task force. Affordable and nutritional food is part of the solution. Across America, green lunchrooms serve fresh food cooked from scratch. These lunchrooms are also composting and recycling. In Baltimore, Maryland, city schools have their own 33-acre (13-ha) organic farm called the Great Kids Farm. The farm provides kids with the opportunity to see how food is grown, and according to Tony Geraci, food service director for Baltimore City Public Schools, "how they can make better choices to change the way things work."

PROS

1. Leftover food is composted, and from it, new produce can grow.
2. Biodegradable cups, utensils, and paper mean no waste will be taken to landfills.
3. School gardens educate children about seasonal produce.

CONS

1. Environmentally friendly cafeterias are expensive to set up.
2. Organic food is difficult to obtain.
3. Some children might not like fresh food.

WORDS TO KNOW

antibiotics: substances that can kill or inactivate bacteria in a living thing

biodegradable: capable of safely breaking down through the natural action of the environment or living things

carbon dioxide: a heavy, colorless gas that forms when fossil fuels burn

carbon footprint: a measure of greenhouse gases produced by human activities

community garden: a piece of land gardened by a group of people together

community supported agriculture (CSA): a partnership between a community and a farmer; individuals buy shares in the crop a farm produces and receive a box of fruit and vegetables each week during the farming season

compost: partially decomposed plant material, such as kitchen waste, used to enrich the soil

emissions: harmful substances discharged in the air, such as exhaust from cars

fair trade: a market-based program that helps pay producers in developing countries fair prices and promote sustainable farming practices

fertilizer: a substance used to increase a soil's ability to grow plants

food cooperative (co-op): a grocery store run by its members

food miles: the distance food travels from the farmer's field to a person's plate

fossil fuels: fuels, such as coal, oil, or natural gas, that were formed hundreds of millions of years ago from plant and animal remains

gene: the basic unit capable of transmitting traits from one generation to the next

global warming: an increase in Earth's average temperature that may be caused by the greenhouse effect

greenhouse gases: gases, such as carbon dioxide and methane, that trap heat when released into the atmosphere

hormones: human-made or natural chemicals that regulate growth and development

landfills: trash disposal sites where waste is buried between layers of earth

methane: a potent greenhouse gas that occurs both naturally and through human activities

organic: relating to food produced without the use of chemicals such as antibiotics or pesticides

pesticides: chemicals used to kill pests

recycle: to process waste material so that it can be used again

renewable: referring to a source of energy that cannot be used up, such as such as solar or wind energy

rotate: to vary crops grown on the same land mostly to keep the soil productive

sustainability: the careful use of natural resources so they are not used up or permanently damaged

INDEX

Log on to www.av2books.com

AV² by Weigl brings you media enhanced books that support active learning. Go to **www.av2books.com**, and enter the special code inside the front cover of this book. You will gain access to enriched and enhanced content that supplements and complements this book. Content includes video, audio, web links, quizzes, a slide show, and activities.

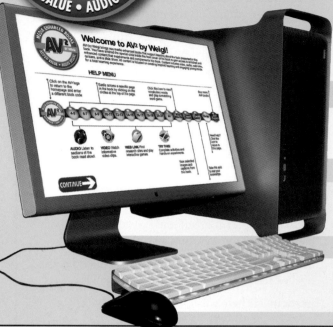

Audio
Listen to sections of the book read aloud.

Video
Watch informative video clips.

Web Link
Find research sites and play interactive games.

Try This!
Complete activities and hands-on experiments.

WHAT'S ONLINE?

Try This! Complete activities and hands-on experiments.	**Web Link** Find research sites and play interactive games.	**Video** Watch informative video clips.	**EXTRA FEATURES**
Pages 12-13 Try this activity about growing your own food.	**Pages 8-9** Learn more about eating local.	**Pages 4-5** Watch a video about eating green.	 **Audio** Hear introductory audi at the top of every pag
Pages 16-17 Complete an activity about reducing kitchen waste.	**Pages 10-11** Link to more information about eating in season.	**Pages 14-15** View a video about green eating ideas.	**Key Words** Study vocabulary, and play a matching word game.
Pages 26-27 Test your knowledge of organic agricultural land.	**Pages 14-15** Find out more about organic food standards.	**Pages 20-21** Learn more about green standards.	**Slide Show** View images and captions, and try a writing activity.
Pages 30 Complete the activity in the book, and then try creating your own debate.	**Pages 28-29** Learn more about green careers.		**AV² Quiz** Take this quiz to test your knowledge